WINERY DOGS

OF SONOMA

Photography by **Andrea Jacoby & Heather Zundel**

Text by **Elaine Riordan**

Published by Winery Dogs Publishing
Hardcover, First Edition
First printing October 2006

ISBN: 0-9773041-2-4

Address correspondence or orders to:
Winery Dogs Publishing
sales@winerydogs.com

Individual books may be purchased at:
www.winerydogs.com

Photography by Andrea Jacoby and Heather Zundel
Foreword by Andrea Jacoby
Text by Elaine Riordan

Design by:

Createffects
(404) 921-3338

Kristin McKee

Printed in Korea by Asianprinting.com

This book is dedicated to Mac, the newest member of our family.

Moose
B.R. Cohn Winery

Winery Dogs of Sonoma

TABLE OF CONTENTS

6 MAP OF SONOMA

9 FOREWORD

CHAPTERS:

10 ALEXANDER VALLEY / CHALK HILL

30 DRY CREEK VALLEY

76 RUSSIAN RIVER VALLEY

120 SONOMA CARNEROS / SONOMA COAST

136 SONOMA VALLEY / SONOMA MOUNTAIN

168 WINERY LISTING

174 OUTTAKES

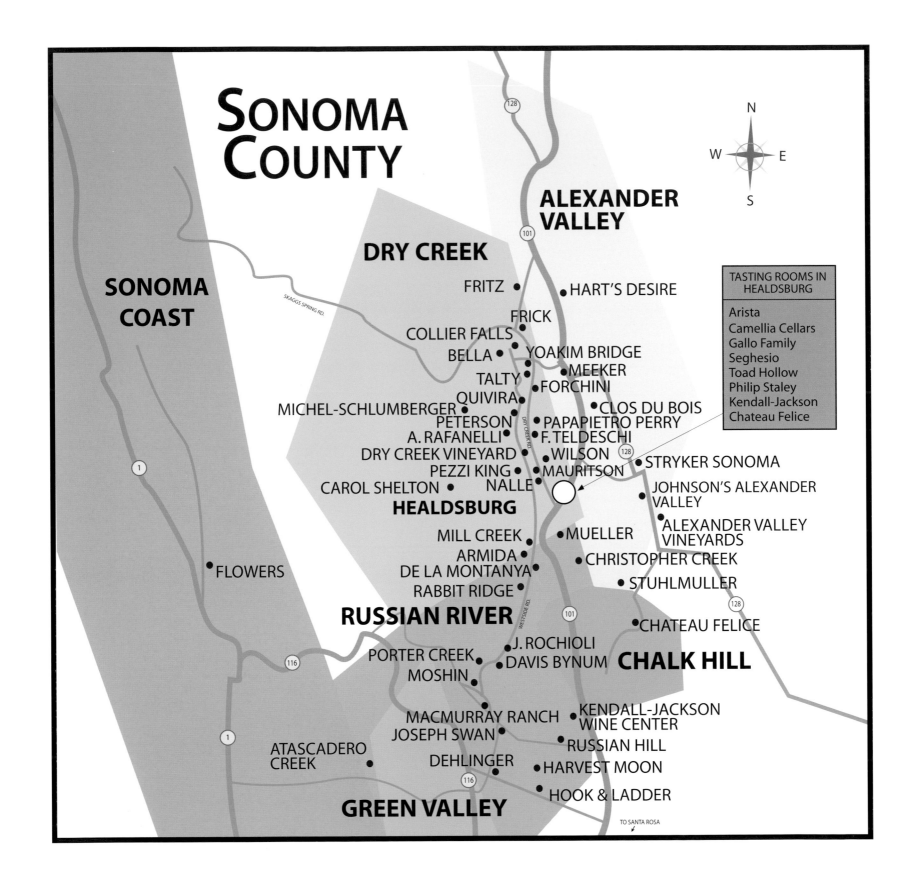

SONOMA COUNTY

SONOMA COAST

DRY CREEK

ALEXANDER VALLEY

SKAGGS SPRING RD.

FRITZ • • HART'S DESIRE

FRICK •

COLLIER FALLS •

BELLA • • YOAKIM BRIDGE

TALTY • • MEEKER

QUIVIRA • • FORCHINI

MICHEL-SCHLUMBERGER •

PETERSON • • CLOS DU BOIS

A. RAFANELLI • • PAPAPIETRO PERRY

DRY CREEK VINEYARD • • F. TELDESCHI

PEZZI KING • • WILSON

CAROL SHELTON • • MAURITSON

NALLE • • STRYKER SONOMA

HEALDSBURG

JOHNSON'S ALEXANDER VALLEY

ALEXANDER VALLEY VINEYARDS

MILL CREEK • • MUELLER

ARMIDA • • CHRISTOPHER CREEK

DE LA MONTANYA •

RABBIT RIDGE • • STUHLMULLER

RUSSIAN RIVER

• CHATEAU FELICE

CHALK HILL

• J. ROCHIOLI

PORTER CREEK • • DAVIS BYNUM

MOSHIN •

MACMURRAY RANCH • • KENDALL-JACKSON WINE CENTER

JOSEPH SWAN • • RUSSIAN HILL

ATASCADERO CREEK • • HARVEST MOON

DEHLINGER •

• HOOK & LADDER

GREEN VALLEY

TO SANTA ROSA

FLOWERS •

TASTING ROOMS IN HEALDSBURG

Arista
Camellia Cellars
Gallo Family
Seghesio
Toad Hollow
Philip Staley
Kendall-Jackson
Chateau Felice

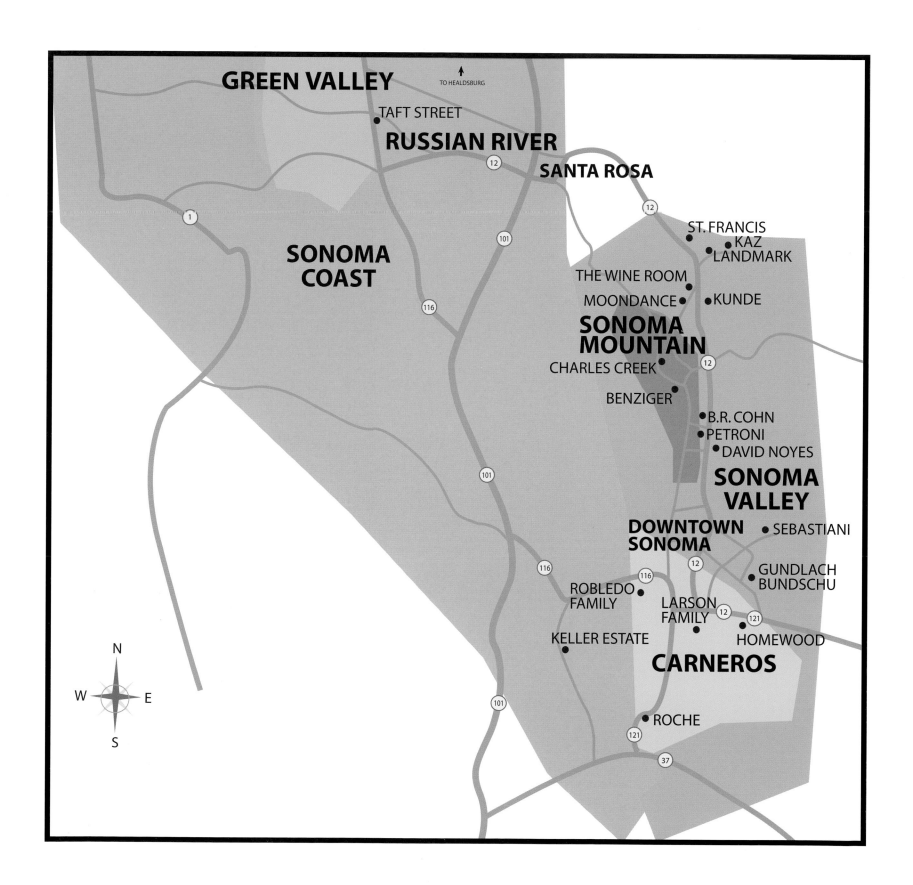

GREEN VALLEY

TO HEALDSBURG

TAFT STREET

RUSSIAN RIVER

12

SANTA ROSA

12

ST. FRANCIS

KAZ

LANDMARK

THE WINE ROOM

MOONDANCE

KUNDE

SONOMA
MOUNTAIN

SONOMA
COAST

1

101

116

CHARLES CREEK

12

BENZIGER

B.R. COHN

PETRONI

DAVID NOYES

SONOMA
VALLEY

101

DOWNTOWN
SONOMA

SEBASTIANI

12

GUNDLACH
BUNDSCHU

116

116

ROBLEDO
FAMILY

LARSON
FAMILY

12

121

KELLER ESTATE

HOMEWOOD

N

CARNEROS

W   E

S

101

ROCHE

121

37

Henry
Nalle Winery

FOREWORD

My husband, Allen, and I were so excited about the success of our first book, *Winery Dogs of Napa Valley*, that we couldn't wait to start a second book in Sonoma. I had been experiencing withdrawal symptoms since my incredible time in Napa, and I knew Sonoma's vineyards and dogs would be just as inspirational. In Sonoma, we found everything we wanted: eye-catching landscapes, excellent light, and, most importantly, a variety of exuberant dogs. As we drove alongside miles of rivers and lakes, out to the ocean, through one-lane bridges, and past endless green farms in the hills, we knew we had found the depth of scenery we were hoping for.

In Sonoma, we discovered, many of the dogs have close interactions with other animals on the winery property. Dogs in all parts of Sonoma are happy to hang out with indoor and outdoor cats, Bantham chickens, miniature horses, standard horses, sheep, llamas, and even Watusi cattle. And when the dogs need a break from the heat or the crowds, many of them have access to water for invigorating swims–whether it's an irrigation lake, the Russian River, or any number of pools and fountains on the property.

Wherever we went, we were welcomed warmly by tasting room employees, winery owners, winemakers, and vineyard managers. We were impressed by the number of tiny wineries and the familial atmosphere at the larger ones. We were given water and delicious wine when we were thirsty, cheese and crackers when we were hungry, barrel tastings, winery tours, vineyard tours, and even sweaters when the famous cool Sonoma nights came on suddenly during a shoot. To name just a few memorable moments of the many I experienced in Sonoma, I will never forget hiking down to the breathtaking waterfall with Barry Collier at Collier Falls, riding in a truck with Brendan Roche and Michael Carr on Roche's estate and watching the dogs leap out toward the lake, picnicking beside the vines at Moshin with the wonderful Moshin family as the sun set, sharing Tocai Frulani with David and Grace Noyes during an intimate interview at their home, barrel tasting Fritz's Syrah with Christina Pallmann, drinking just-released Pinot Gris at 9 a.m. at the spacious MacMurray Ranch as Kate MacMurray welcomed us, and enjoying an extensive winery luncheon at Kendall-Jackson with a huge, happy group of family and friends as all the puppies played together. Every day we were in Sonoma, we knew how lucky we were.

In my last book I chose to use only the wine labels featuring dogs. For Sonoma, however, I decided to feature a label for every winery in the book. Wine labels just keep getting more elegant, and they convey the beauty and spirit of the wineries they represent. As the book's pages came together during the design process, I enjoyed seeing how the photographs of the dogs and the labels gave the pages new colors, balance, and feeling.

The people of Sonoma will always hold a special place in my heart for their gracious hospitality and genuine interest in our endeavor. Allen and I have learned more than we ever imagined about life in the wine country. In fact, our passion for wine grew so much that we had to invest in a cellar to contain the fantastic wine we've discovered along this journey. We would like to thank everyone for opening their doors wide for us and letting us learn about the wineries, taste all the amazing wine, and interact with these joyful dogs. I don't think I'm spoiling any secrets when I say that Sonoma is a gorgeous, warm, fascinating place, and I will always be grateful for the insider's view of Sonoma's wine country.

Alexander Valley

Alexander Valley Vineyards

Clos du Bois

Hart's Desire Wines

Johnson's Alexander Valley Wines

Meeker Vineyard

Seghesio Family Vineyards

Stryker Sonoma Winery & Vineyards

Stuhlmuller Vineyards

Chalk Hill

Chateau Felice

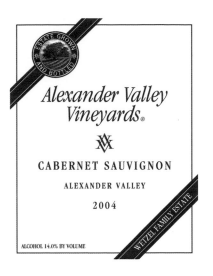

Mattie (left) &
Susie

SUSIE, CASEY & MATTIE
ALEXANDER VALLEY VINEYARDS

Three generations—Susie (age twelve), Casey (four), and Mattie (seven months)—live easygoing lives at the winery. Most days Susie stays home enjoying peace and solitude while Casey, who's very obedient, and Mattie, who's very sweet, retrieve sticks in the vineyard and barrel bungs in the cool cave. But the three yellow Labrador retrievers are happiest when they pile into the pickup truck and take off with winery owners Hank and Linda Wetzel to the Russian River. On hot summer days, the Wetzels bring a picnic and the dogs leap into the eddy for floating sticks. The tireless dogs bring the sticks back to shore again and again, until Hank tells them it's time to head home. "It makes me happy to give them a free environment," says Hank. "Here they can live without being tethered and locked up, and they're happy."

Casey

MORA, NADIE, BAILEY & BINGO
CLOS DU BOIS

Mora (left),
Bailey & Nadie

Bingo

At Clos du Bois, a dog-friendly winery to employees and guests alike, the dogs are distinct individuals, flourishing in their different domains. Mora, a ten-year-old dingo/blue healer mix, has a talent for climbing and jumping—she can even pursue a squirrel forty feet up an oak tree. Viticulturist Douglas Price, who worries about her fearlessness, tries to distract her from trees by enticing her to jump into his arms. Seven-year-old Nadie is a gentle yellow Labrador retriever/golden retriever mix, says vineyard manager Keith Horn. Her training to visit hospital patients carries over to her kind interactions with guests. Away from the crowd, Nadie romps in the river and plays hide-and-seek with her rubber duckie. Bailey, a two-year-old chocolate Labrador retriever, is the perfect office assistant for bulk wine manager Julian Slee. When he's not arranging and rearranging Julian's paperwork, he's running faxes around the office and fetching Julian's phone, which is mysteriously full of holes and scratches. Bingo, the "ranch dog," is a yellow Labrador retriever of unknown age. Left behind by a vineyard worker, the lovable Bingo gets food, care, and affection from the vineyard crew.

Mora (front), Nadie (left) & Bailey

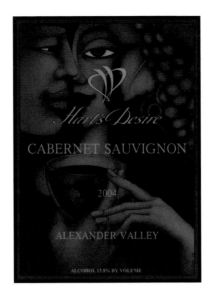

ANNIE
HART'S DESIRE WINES

Annie, an eleven-year-old Labrador retriever/golden retriever mix, does not chase cats or birds, does not hunt, and does not like water. In fact, winery owners John and Desiré Hart say that during the rare times she's gone into the Russian River, she looks like a huge praying mantis. Instead, Annie is almost entirely a social being, assuming every guest has arrived specifically to see her. At home on Hidden Spring Vineyard, Annie follows John everywhere, and when she's hot, John cools her down with a hose and watches her roll in her favorite grassy spot before she rejoins him in the rows. During winemaking, she enjoys juice from the small basket press, especially late harvest Zinfandel. In the evenings, when John and Desiré are drinking their renowned Cabernet Sauvignon, she'll wander over to drink her share from their glasses.

GRETCHEN, CASEY, EDDIE & IZZY
JOHNSON'S ALEXANDER VALLEY WINES

*Eddie (left) &
Casey*

Winery owner, winemaker, and dog breeder Ellen Johnson says that basset hounds are stubborn, independent, and very smart. They're also great rabbit chasers in the vineyard and fine company in the tasting room. Gretchen, seven years old, is not a mother but is a protective aunt. If the old winery cat, Patch, chases the puppies, Auntie Gretchen chases Patch. Casey, six years old, is a champion dog and a "counter surfer"; he's even turned on Ellen's stove burners in search of food. Eddie, one year old, still acts like a puppy but has already won several contests dressed as Elvis, complete with fabulous wigs and guitars. Izzy, just six months old, is sweet and accommodating, enjoying the company of all people and dogs. The younger winery cat, Bart, approaches the dogs often, rubbing up against them and licking their large, endearing faces.

Casey (front), Gretchen
(left), Eddie & Izzy

ABIGAIL, EPPIE, GINGER & MOOSE
MEEKER VINEYARD

Eppie

Moose

Abigail, Eppie, Ginger, and Moose love to go to work with winery owners Charlie and Molly Meeker. Eppie, a cairn terrier, insists on visiting the tasting room with Molly to meet new people. Known as "the bionic dog," Eppie was once hit by a Suburban, resulting in a hip replacement, but she's still going strong at age fifteen. Charlie takes Ginger, Moose, and Abigail to the winery. Ginger (not pictured), a fourteen-year-old mixed breed, is shy but a good pointer. Ginger's son, Moose, a six-year-old chocolate Labrador retriever mix, is the bravest in the bunch. Abigail, a two-year-old Greater Swiss Mountain dog and an international champion, is "127 pounds of sugar and spice." Outside, she herds the other dogs by nipping at their heels. Inside, she's a lap dog who goes nose-to-nose with the Meekers.

VITO
SEGHESIO FAMILY VINEYARDS

Vito, a five-year-old black Labrador retriever, used to be "a real mover," says winery patriarch Ed Seghesio. A classic wanderer, Vito could end up a mile from home, and friends and neighbors would pick him up and drive him back. These days, however, whenever Vito goes out the dog door, he barks for Ed to come out and play. Ed obliges, tossing him tennis balls—which Vito never misses—and then he starts up the truck. Vito runs beside the truck as far as the Russian River, and then he swims nonstop until Ed calls him back. At the office, Vito keeps Ed company throughout the day. At night, Vito shares a huge, comfortable loveseat with Minx, the cuddly, gray family cat.

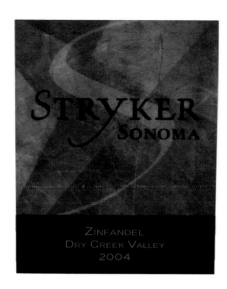

MACS
STRYKER SONOMA WINERY & VINEYARDS

Every morning Macs, a two-year-old Labradoodle, struts out on his home's big rock wall, looking out over his domain as if he's on the battlefield. Let loose in the vineyard, he chases rabbits nonstop, pausing briefly only to eat a few grapes. When Macs' mom and dad, Karen and Craig MacDonald, take the four-wheeler through the vineyard rows, Macs runs alongside them, never getting tired. Sweet and curious, he's the perfect protector for the kids and mellow companion for Craig and Karen. "Overall, we've always thought that wine tasting should be fun and educational, not intimidating, and a dog like Macs illustrates this perfectly," says Karen. "We want people to feel welcome at Stryker Sonoma, and nothing does that better than a greeting from a friendly dog like Macs."

2005
Stuhlmuller Vineyards

ESTATE
CHARDONNAY
Alexander Valley

ALCOHOL 14.3% BY VOLUME

Since 1982 our family has been growing chardonnay grapes along the banks of the Russian River where clockwork fog and cool afternoon breezes allow for slow, gentle ripening of the fruit. Located at the meeting place of three renowned appellations — Alexander Valley, Chalk Hill and the Russian River Valley — Stuhlmuller Vineyards' unique combination of site, soil and vine selection produces wines of depth and sophistication. To enjoy the full richness and charm of our estate chardonnay, we suggest serving it lightly chilled, but not cold.

HUNTER
STUHLMULLER VINEYARDS

Hunter, an eleven-year-old chocolate Labrador retriever, wakes up at 6:30 a.m. every day for her morning cookie. If winemaker Leo Hansen doesn't get up immediately, she dances around the bed. Sometimes, on a very hot day, Leo imagines that she'd be happier resting at home with the three cats, one of whom is a great friend. But just as he starts to leave, Hunter hangs her head sadly at the gate, and Leo often can't help but change his mind. When Leo's inside the winery, she's inside, too. When Leo's at the tanks, she's at the tanks, too. She swims in the river, eats Chardonnay and Cabernet Sauvignon grapes off the ground, and plays gently with any visiting dog. In the winter, she naps in the back seat of Leo's car. Mellow, devoted, and full of good energy, "Hunter keeps the spirit up," Leo says.

Felice

FELICE & SKETCHER
CHATEAU FELICE

Sketcher

Felice

Winery owners Phyllis and Barry Rodgers are thrilled that their family business is such a success. Luckily, their daughters—Genevieve Llerena, the winemaker, and Samantha Rodgers, the tasting room manager—picked two perfect dogs to help the winery run so well. Felice, a nine-year-old black Labrador retriever/Weimaraner mix, and Sketcher, a nine-year-old English cocker spaniel, chase rabbits from the vines, accompany the family at the crusher pad, and enjoy interacting with guests. Only Felice can swim (Sketcher, "the party dog," once took a flying leap into the water and had to be rescued), but both respect the two geese who swim peacefully in the chateau's beautiful lower lake. "The dogs fit the place," says Phyllis. "They bring love to the wine every day."

Dry Creek Valley

A. Rafanelli Winery

Armida Winery

Bella Vineyards & Wine Caves

Camellia Cellars

Carol Shelton Wines

Collier Falls Vineyards

Dry Creek Vineyard

F. Teldeschi Winery

Forchini Vineyards & Winery

Frick Winery

Fritz Winery

Mauritson Wines

Michel-Schlumberger Wine Estate

Mill Creek Vineyards & Winery

Nalle Winery

Papapietro Perry Winery

Peterson Winery

Pezzi King Vineyards

Quivira Vineyards

Talty Vineyards & Winery

Wilson Winery

Yoakim Bridge Vineyards & Winery

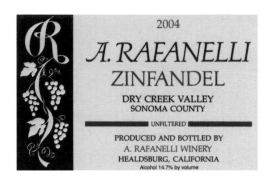

2004
A. RAFANELLI
ZINFANDEL
DRY CREEK VALLEY
SONOMA COUNTY

UNFILTERED

PRODUCED AND BOTTLED BY
A. RAFANELLI WINERY
HEALDSBURG, CALIFORNIA
Alcohol 14.7% by volume

BODIE & MILO
A. RAFANELLI WINERY

Milo (left) &
Bodie

Bodie and his son Milo, ages nine and five, enjoy their lives at the winery all year long. In spring and summer, the two yellow Labrador retrievers run down the winery's long driveway to greet guests and take breaks swimming in the nearby pond. One year Milo got into the pond's floating goose house and carefully swam back with a goose egg in his mouth, showing off to the laughing crowd. At harvest, the two dogs walk beneath the fermenters, lapping up wine and getting stained and sticky. At Halloween, winemaker Shelly Rafanelli-Fehlman dresses them up in elaborate costumes—they're already famous for their past disguises as pirates, bumblebees, special ops, and pimps. When winter approaches, they pose with Shelly and the rest of the family for the winery's popular Christmas cards and, freed from the limelight, run out to greet holiday visitors.

Bodie (front) &
Milo

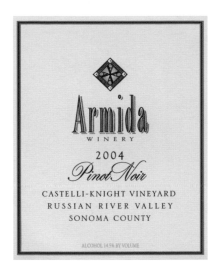

2004
Pinot Noir
CASTELLI-KNIGHT VINEYARD
RUSSIAN RIVER VALLEY
SONOMA COUNTY

ALCOHOL 14.5% BY VOLUME

SAGE
ARMIDA WINERY

Armida Winery has a strong connection to animal shelters. Not only does the winery raise funds for Healdsburg's animal shelter, but winery owners—and brothers—Steve and Bruce Cousins always have a rescue dog on the property. Past winery dogs Diva and Wino had the run of the property and constant affection. Wino was especially outgoing, greeting every guest and trailing the employees as they worked. Sage, a five-year-old husky mix, is a bit shy, but, as Bruce says, "Wino's spirit lives on through Sage." Like Wino before her, Sage warmly greets customers and poses meaningfully on the cool tasting room floor, garnering the guests' appreciation as they sip specialty wines. At Armida's expansive picnic area, Sage greets guests table by table. Then she's off to the pond, where she swims and chases after ducks, egrets, and any other birds visiting the property.

MOLLY
BELLA VINEYARDS & WINE CAVES

Gentle and mellow, Molly, an eleven-year-old Border collie, is the ultimate guest escort. When guests arrive, she meets them at their cars, leads them to the cave, and then waits patiently outside the giant cave doors as they taste single-vineyard Zinfandel and Syrah. When guests reemerge, she walks them back to their cars, generally with a long stick in her mouth. During one winery event in the caves, Molly was uncharacteristically without a stick. Luckily, an old Zinfandel vine was decorating the wall, and to everyone's amusement, Molly deftly snapped off a limb for herself. Wine club director Timothy Nordvedt says Molly is persistent, but never aggressive, when someone takes her stick away. She crouches down and sneaks slowly toward it until she can claim her prize.

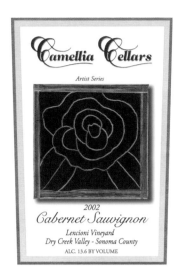

2002
Cabernet Sauvignon
Lencioni Vineyard
Dry Creek Valley - Sonoma County
ALC. 13.6 BY VOLUME

ARCHIE
CAMELLIA CELLARS

"More people know Archie than they know us," says winemaker Bruce Snyder, and it's no wonder: Archie, an eight-year-old golden retriever, is a dog about town. At seven months old, he was hit by a car and paralyzed for three months. Thanks to hot tub therapy with Bruce and winery owner Chris Lewand, Archie regained his strength and happiness. Known as the $10,000 dog because of the veterinary expenses, he's been a worthwhile investment— people stop along the road just to pet him, and he often leads them into the tasting room. When the UPS and FedEx drivers arrive, he jumps into their trucks for treats. One day, the FedEx driver was two blocks away before he saw Archie's head pop up in the back. To further increase Archie's popularity, Archie's "Uncle Mario," a family friend, takes him to the local bars in town, where there's always an old friend to greet and a new friend anxious to meet him.

Troi

Winery Dogs of Sonoma

Rocky

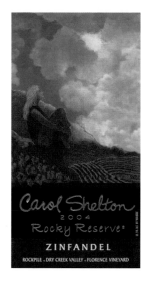

TROI, MONGA, WILEY & ROCKY
CAROL SHELTON WINES

Wiley

The four longhaired standard dachshunds in winemaker and president Carol Shelton's home are intimately connected with each other. The fourteen-year-old Troi (who inspired Black Magic, Carol's late-harvest Zinfandel) gave birth, at age ten, to her own "late harvest": Monga, Wiley, and Rocky. Monga (not pictured), named after Carol's Monga Zin, is easygoing, quite a talker, and very affectionate—kissing people on the eyeballs. Wiley, named after Carol's Wild Thing, is obsessed with food and females and is the biggest in the group. Rocky, named after the Rocky Reserve, is known as the "rocket scientist"—he quickly learned to drink from the outside faucet and taught all the others by example. At wine events, customers ask not only to taste Carol's award-winning wine but to see her latest photos of the four gorgeous dogs.

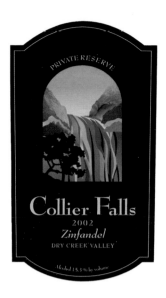

LUCY
COLLIER FALLS VINEYARDS

L ucy, an eight-year-old yellow Labrador retriever, started her life in the wrong home. Fortunately, the mother of two who'd adopted her realized that Lucy was not happy in the apartment, and she put an ad in the paper. When winery owners Barry and Susan Collier arrived to meet Lucy, they saw the energetic puppy pulling hard on her leash—with two small kids barely holding on—and said to each other, "She's ours." Today, rain or shine, Lucy spends her days running in the vineyard. She runs alongside the ATVs and trucks, barking and barking until Barry throws her a ball to hold in her mouth. At the winery's signature waterfall, Lucy swims in the clear, cool spring and fetches sticks for hours, showing everyone that she's found the perfect home.

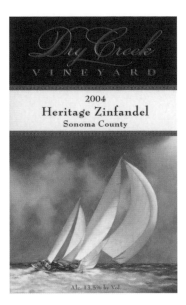

2004
Heritage Zinfandel
Sonoma County

Alc. 13.5% by Vol.

TRUMAN
DRY CREEK VINEYARD

Truman, a nine-month-old golden retriever, was the biggest dog in the litter, but even today he's not aware of his size. Still in "puppy mode," as director of communications Bill Smart says, Truman runs wildly—even in very hot weather—and joyfully jumps on people to greet them. Most days he stays in the office with Bill, with frequent breaks to run with abandon on the property. At home on his front steps in Healdsburg, Truman is an avid people watcher. Instead of barking, Truman greets people by jumping up on the fence and leaning on his front paws, waiting excitedly to be petted.

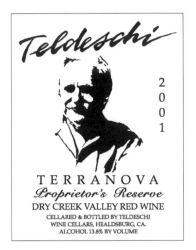

ROSCO
F. TELDESCHI WINERY

At six weeks old, Rosco, an English springer spaniel, looked like a Guinea pig, says vineyard manager John Teldeschi. He was an adorable runt, riding around in the back of their son Lucas's remote-control truck. Over the next two years, he grew into a busy winery dog—riding on four-wheelers, hunting for lizards and moles, and sharing tacos with the vineyard crews. He was also a competent watchdog, barking at wild turkeys and looking out for Lucas and his sister, Sophia. Then John and Robin Teldeschi brought Matthew home, and Rosco changed. Matthew was the first baby Rosco had seen, and he suddenly became Matthew's ultimate protector. UPS and FedEx drivers were seen as threats, and Rosco got upset if anyone sat too close to Matthew. When a crowd gathered to see the baby, Rosco forcefully herded them away. Today, at age four, Rosco still doesn't trust strangers, but he's generally more relaxed, eating grapes off the vine and anything else he can find.

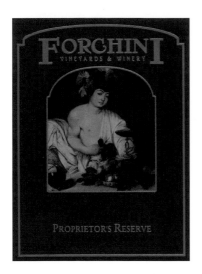

TUFF, CALI, GINA, SOPHIE & LUCY
FORCHINI VINEYARDS & WINERY

Lucy

Sophie

The Forchini dogs are a happy crew, and each has a distinct talent. Tuff, an eight-year-old yellow Labrador retriever, protects other creatures. If he sees a cat with a live mouse, he'll tell the cat to drop it and then stand guard until Francie Forchini comes to the rescue. Tuff's cousin Cali, a five-year-old yellow Labrador retriever, brings the newspaper into the house every day. If the paper's not on the property, she's not undone–she'll just bring in the neighbor's. Gina, a five-year-old chocolate Labrador retriever, chases rabbits from the vines, row by row. The five-year-old Catahoula hound, Sophie, builds a nest of leaves and twigs every spring and fills it with the wild turkey eggs she finds. Lucy, a four-year-old Labrador retriever mix, is the most mischievous, sneaking into the tasting room to revel in the attention the guests inevitably give her.

Gina (front), Cali (left) & Tuff

LUCIA & MADISON
FRICK WINERY

2003 Dry Creek Valley
Gannon Vineyard, Estate Bottled
Viognier
facing down the hillside
the world is new

PRODUCED & BOTTLED BY FRICK WINERY, B.W. 4771
23072 WALLING RD., GEYSERVILLE, CALIFORNIA USA
Alcohol by Volume 14.2%

Madison

Winery owner and winemaker Bill Frick works the winery by himself—working the vineyard, making the wine, and running the tasting room. That's why Lucia and Madison, both nine years old, are indispensable to Bill's success. Lucia, an old English sheepdog/golden retriever mix, herds customers into the tasting room, where Lucia's portrait—painted by Bill's late wife, Judith Gannon—hangs behind the bar. Madison, or "Maddie," a golden retriever, was rescued by Bill's partner, Dallas Saunders. A gifted landscape designer, Maddie rips apart stuffed animals and artistically strews their disembodied limbs across the property. She also likes to refresh visitors by diving into creeks and shaking water on them. When Lucia and Maddie are not wowing guests, they frolic together in the mud and relax with Lucky, the laid-back winery cat.

Lucia

CHANCE
FRITZ WINERY

Chancellor, or "Chance," is an eight-year-old golden retriever mix who shows no signs of slowing down. Chance's favorite part of the day is the morning, when winemaker Christina Pallmann inspects the vines. As soon as they arrive at a vineyard, Chance jumps out of the truck and races through the rows, terrifying rabbits, gophers, and deer. In fact, he's developed such a strong reputation for relentlessly pursuing deer that local vineyard owners with deer problems issue him special invitations to visit. Since Christina is his chauffeur, she's allowed along as well. But for all Chance's energy, there are two things that keep him still—a truck ride and the opportunity to lounge in the office, resting up for the next vineyard run.

SOHO
MAURITSON WINES

Soho, a three-year-old yellow Labrador retriever, took to life as a winery dog when she arrived at Mauritson at six weeks old. In no time her favorite toys were silicon wine bungs, which she enjoyed pulling out of wine barrels. A spirited runner, Soho used to run in circles so fast that winery owner Clay Mauritson stubbed his toes chasing her, one time breaking his foot in three places. These days, after a litter of eleven puppies, she is a mellower presence, following Clay wherever he goes and greeting customers in the tasting room. Her puppies are so beautiful that more than a hundred people are on the waiting list to adopt them.

LUKE
MICHEL-SCHLUMBERGER WINE ESTATE

"Luke disarms people," says winery president Jacques Schlumberger. Luke's undeniable charisma draws people to the winery, encouraging conversations, good feeling, and sales. A Tibetan terrier, from a breed developed to be gentle companion dogs for Tibetan monks, Luke was rescued from the streets in San Francisco. Today, Luke has found his true companions in Jacques and Barbara. At Barbara's psychotherapy practice, he is always a calming presence. During public events at the winery, his innate ability to charm a crowd results in delicious treats from numerous plates.

DANTE
MILL CREEK VINEYARDS & WINERY

In front of a lovely, converted old barn, near a replica mill pond and wheel, Dante—a three-year-old Alaskan malamute/white German shepherd mix—loves the chase. He chases squirrels and birds on the property, and he never tires of chasing Clyde, the longsuffering winery cat. When he's feeling more sociable, he functions as the winery's customer relations coordinator, circulating among the guests and licking the face of every willing admirer. He also pals around with his friend Sage, a husky mix who lives at Armida Winery, and together they dig for gophers and nap in the sun. At the end of the day, Brian Kreck, the winery's special events coordinator, takes Dante home for a well-earned dinner and a good night's sleep at his comfortable doghouse.

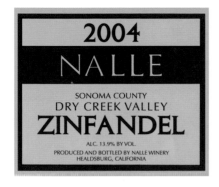

SOLO & HENRY
NALLE WINERY

Solo

Solo, a thirteen-year-old yellow Labrador retriever, was raised by two different families, enjoying lively outings and relaxing days in a quiet neighborhood. After proprietors Doug and Lee Nalle adopted her, she immediately became "the Lab in the lab," finding her own indoor spot for sleeping. In the cellar/tasting room, she's happy to lie in the middle of the crowd, forcing people to step over and around her. She'll eat grapes and anything else she can find, but she won't drink water from a bowl, preferring to drink it from puddles, a hose, or the bottoms of flower pots. Henry, a ten-year-old American Staffordshire terrier, is a wanderer, roaming free in the vineyard and interacting with people at a nearby house. The life of the party in the tasting room, Henry draws a crowd and makes people happy. As Andrew Nalle, assistant winemaker, says, "Henry brings good energy to us, and he makes sure the winemaking atmosphere is not so serious. He's like us—silly, different, and cool."

Henry

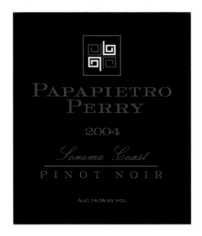

PAPAPIETRO
PERRY

2004

Sonoma Coast

PINOT NOIR

ALC 14.5% BY VOL.

RUBY
PAPAPIETRO PERRY WINERY

"Winery dogs are critical to making customers feel at ease," says Renae Perry, who owns the winery with her husband, Bruce, and partners Ben and Yolanda Papapietro. "Most customers are on vacation, and they miss their pets. So when they see a dog at the winery, they feel a little closer to home." Ruby, a six-year-old chocolate Labrador retriever/chow mix, can make anyone feel welcome. She greets all approaching customers, barking with excitement, and is in heaven if anyone throws a ball for her retrieval. When the winery hours end, Ruby follows Renae and Bruce inside and outside the winery, checking barrels and vines, and when it's time for paperwork, Ruby sleeps soundly under Renae's desk.

BEBE
PETERSON WINERY

Beryl Buncrana—known as "BeBe"—is a seven-year-old Norfolk terrier who was a champion show dog in Connecticut before moving to California. Adopted several years ago by a wine country family, she loves her less structured life at the winery. She grooms herself like a cat, plays with a variety of squeaky toys, and sleeps so fervently that winery owner Fred Peterson calls her a "sleep hound." While indifferent to other dogs and interested in humans only when they have food, horses are a different story. Norfolk terriers were bred to be stable dogs, and BeBe's instinct is strong. Whenever she sees horses, in a stable or out to pasture, she stares at them for a long time and then approaches them quietly, happy simply to be beside them.

Riley

Monty

MONTY & RILEY
PEZZI KING VINEYARDS

Monty and Riley, the inspirations for the Scottie Club at Pezzi King, are excellent photography models and companions for winery owners Jim and Cynthia Rowe. Monty, an eleven-year-old Wheaten Scottish terrier, graced the artwork on the winery's Muscat dessert wine. When the wine quickly sold out, customers called just to get the empty bottles. Monty enjoys relaxing on the couch until he hears the barbecue fire up—and then he runs to see what's cooking. Riley, a three-year-old Wheaten Scottish terrier, is featured on the Riley's Red Zinfandel label. Friendly and curious, he attends all tastings and barbecues. Riley loves to antagonize the winery's miniature horses, Snickers and Tinkerbell, but because he also loves to nip at their heels, Cynthia keeps him out of the pen. Luckily, the steady stream of admiring guests keeps him occupied.

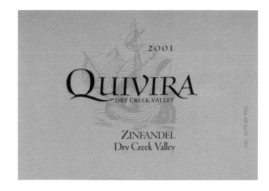

SOPHIE
QUIVIRA VINEYARDS

S ophie, a three-year-old rottweiler, is a gentle dog and a great protector. Vineyard manager Tony Castellanos and his wife, Rita, take their daughters to the Russian River, and Sophie keeps her eye on them. If the girls go out too far, Sophie pulls them out of the water. At the winery's creek, Sophie plays gently with steelhead trout as they swim, never hurting them. When she sees chickens running around, she chases them down and puts them back in their cages. Most days Tony has work to do inside the winery, and he knows he'll find Sophie right outside the door, waiting for him to return to the Zinfandel vines. She especially likes hanging out with all the vineyard workers at lunchtime, enjoying food and good company. On nights when the winery's alarm goes off, Tony drives out to check on the property. With the attentive, loyal Sophie at his side, he knows he's safe.

MAX & CHARLIE
TALTY VINEYARDS & WINERY

Charlie

For ten years, Max—an Australian shepherd/Border collie mix—has used his herding instincts to help winery owners Michael and Katie Talty. Years ago, the Taltys' son Nicholas, then two years old, slipped through the back door, sending the Taltys on a frantic search. Sensing the urgency, Max ran through the electric fence, found Nicholas a quarter-mile away, and waited with him until the Taltys arrived. Today, Max guides guests to the tasting room—if they head the wrong way, Max blocks them from proceeding, then herds them the right way. He naps with a stuffed animal in his mouth and then buries it in Katie's flower garden. Confident in all ways, Max is not sure what to make of Charlie, a thirteen-week-old shih tzu. Charlie follows Max everywhere, something Max isn't used to from a non-human. The Taltys hope that Max won't one day mistake Charlie for one of his stuffed animals!

Max

Mandy (left),
Mindy & Molly

Mindy

MANDY, MOLLY & MINDY
WILSON WINERY

Mandy, Molly, and Mindy eat, nap, and travel together, but they entertain people in their own ways. Mandy, an eleven-year-old Australian shepherd, took top honors in obedience training, says office manager Linda Barnhisel. These days she plays baseball every morning with Linda's grandson, Jeremy—he gets his practice, and Mandy gets her exercise. Molly, a one-year-old Border collie, entertains herself for hours by jumping in the air and chasing leaves. When winery owner Diane Wilson cleans barrels, Molly races over to nip at the running water. Mindy, a three-month-old miniature Australian shepherd, is an energetic puppy devoted to Linda and to her two older canine companions. As soon as the tasting room opens, the three dogs run past the winery's trademark flamingo lawn ornaments to check out the new visitors.

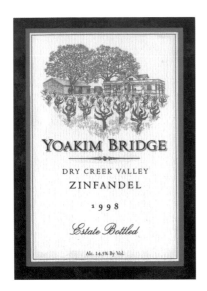

ETHYL & MADALINE
YOAKIM BRIDGE VINEYARDS & WINERY

Madaline

Ethyl

Ethyl, a ten-year-old miniature schnauzer, and Madaline, a ten-year-old old English bulldog, get excited when guests arrive. Ethyl "sounds the alarm," says winery owner Virginia Morgan, and chases cars and buses—the bigger, the better—in the driveway. Madaline wiggles her body uncontrollably, letting the crowds come to her. If anyone has a balloon, she'll bounce it with her nose until she can pop it with her teeth. In the vineyards, Ethyl chases gophers and brings them home to Virginia. Madaline, "the resident architect," pulls canes and logs into a pile on the front lawn, carefully arranging them in a style uniquely her own. During winemaking, as Virginia and winemaker David Cooper punch down, the two dogs sometimes drink too much and suffer mild hangovers in the morning. "We live in a place we love, work with whom we love, and make a product that we are proud of. Life just can't get any better!" says Virginia, as Ethyl barks and Madaline wiggles in obvious agreement.

Russian River Valley

Arista Winery

Atascadero Creek Winery

Christopher Creek Winery

Davis Bynum Winery

Dehlinger Winery

De La Montanya Winery & Vineyards

Harvest Moon Estate & Winery

Hook & Ladder Vineyards and Winery

J. Rochioli Vineyards & Winery

Joseph Swan Vineyards

Kendall-Jackson Wine Estates

MacMurray Ranch

Moshin Vineyards

Mueller Winery

Philip Staley Vineyards & Winery

Porter Creek Vineyards

Rabbit Ridge Vineyards & Winery

Russian Hill Estate Winery

Taft Street Winery

Toad Hollow Vineyards

LUCY
ARISTA WINERY

ARISTA

Russian River Valley Pinot Noir

2003

♣ ♣ ♣

Lucy, a two-year-old Maltese, loves to sunbathe on the deck outside the tasting room, contentedly chewing corks, as she waits for the morning's first customers. As guests stroll through the winery's Japanese water gardens and into the picnic areas, Lucy enjoys tagging along, hoping to taste any food that drops. When it rains, Lucy rolls around in the mud puddles, instantly turning her fluffy white fur into chocolate brown. Despite this transformation, guests continually admire her. Mark McWilliams, director of sales, and Jennifer McWilliams keep a close eye on Lucy to protect her not only from hawks but also from customers trying to add Lucy to their wine purchases.

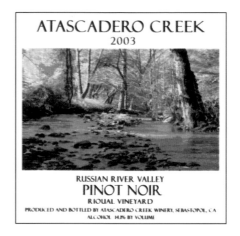

ATASCADERO CREEK
2003

RUSSIAN RIVER VALLEY
PINOT NOIR
RIQUAL VINEYARD
PRODUCED AND BOTTLED BY ATASCADERO CREEK WINERY, SEBASTOPOL, CA
ALCOHOL 14.3% BY VOLUME

ALBERT
ATASCADERO CREEK WINERY

"Albert has no flaws," says winery owner Bob Appleby. "He doesn't dig, wreck, or bark; he doesn't bother the chickens; and he keeps me company all day." A four-year-old golden retriever whose father was a national champion, Albert chases rabbits from the vines and accompanies Bob in his truck during deliveries. In return, Bob kicks little soccer balls for Albert to retrieve among the rows of Pinot Noir grapes in the former railroad right of way. In the winter, Albert's coat grows so long that he resembles a musk ox, and he even gets dreadlocks. But despite his wild appearance, Albert is above all a gentle soul and is at peace with his family at Atascadero Creek.

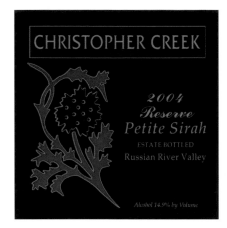

MUKI
CHRISTOPHER CREEK WINERY

As soon as winemaker Chris Russi saw Muki, he knew he'd found a friend. Now a seven-year-old blue healer/terrier mix, Muki has adjusted from the cramped life at a shelter to the free life as a winery dog. She walks beside Chris as he works in the vineyard, greets visitors as their cars pull into the driveway, and suns herself in the picnic area, enjoying the guests' nonstop adoration. When John Scherer, a tasting room employee, arrives for work, Muki races to meet him. Holding a biscuit, John watches Muki's tail wind up to "40 wags per minute" and waits for her to let out her distinctive howl. After more treats and diligent hours of customer service, Muki naps behind the tasting room counter.

DAVIS
BYNUM

2002

RUSSIAN RIVER VALLEY

PINOT NOIR

ALC.13.8% BY VOL.

FRED
DAVIS BYNUM WINERY

Fred, an eight-year-old golden retriever and rescue dog, is known in all the bars in Healdsburg. When he strolls into his favorite establishment, John and Zeke's Bar & Grill, he barks at the boar's head above the bar, crawls under the pool table, and falls asleep. But Davis Bynum, his daughter, Susie, and Susie's daughter, Lindley, know that Fred loves his life best at home. At the winery he trolls the picnic area for scraps and attention, keeps visitors company in the tasting room, and plays with the landscape gardener's golden retriever in the organic vineyards. Companionable and devoted, he naps near Lindley at the office and spends quiet nights with her, content in his life in the Russian River Valley.

2003

DEHLINGER

Pinot Noir

RUSSIAN RIVER VALLEY
ESTATE BOTTLED

PETRA
DEHLINGER WINERY

Petra, a three-year-old Doberman pinscher, races up and down hills, tearing through the winery's Pinot Noir vines at up to twenty-six miles per hour. As gophers scurry in the grass, Petra snorts her way along, immersing her long nose in their burrows. Unaware that she is from a long line of show dogs, Petra loves life on the farm and comes home every night with a dirt-caked nose. Winery owners Tom and Carole Dehlinger appreciate Petra's remarkable athleticism, grace, and sense of humor.

ROSIE
DE LA MONTANYA WINERY & VINEYARDS

The fourth in a series of English springer spaniels for winery owners Tina and Dennis De La Montanya, two-year-old Rosie loves her days in the vineyards. Not only does she chase jackrabbits and birds from the vines, but she understands and obeys the workers' commands in English and Spanish. Though she is friendly to everyone, her best friends are Dennis and Tina's sons, Dean and Dylan, who find Rosie's expert burps endlessly amusing. Her energy and good nature inspire the De La Montanyas to create about twenty distinctively different wines per year, a testament to the vitality of the entire family.

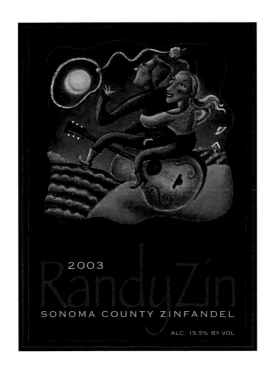

CHARLOTTE
HARVEST MOON ESTATE & WINERY

"I can't tell you what I did before I had Charlotte," says grower and winemaker Randy Pitts. The absolutely necessary two-year-old Chesapeake Bay retriever/chocolate Labrador retriever mix chases gophers from the vines and boosts sales with her sweet disposition and expert greeting abilities. According to Randy's calculations, people buy more wine when Charlotte is there—a fact that isn't taken lightly since nearly all of his sales are through the tasting room. "Dogs reduce the pretentiousness of the industry," Randy says, and Charlotte helps him achieve his goal of encouraging guests to stay awhile, not just taste wines quickly and leave. The winery's latest Zinfandel label features a glowing Charlotte beside Randy and his wife, Kelli Crouch, a happy family who clearly loves the daily life at the winery.

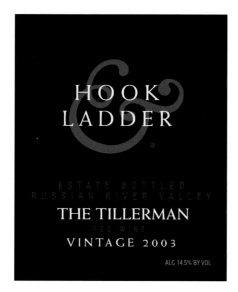

HOOK & LADDER

ESTATE BOTTLED
RUSSIAN RIVER VALLEY
THE TILLERMAN
RED WINE
VINTAGE 2003

ALC 14.5% BY VOL

DAISY
HOOK & LADDER VINEYARDS AND WINERY

Daisy's life with winery owner Cecil De Loach began with high drama. At eight months old, the Labrador retriever mix showed up on Cecil's property foaming at the mouth, and everyone around was afraid she had rabies. Someone even wondered if she should be shot. A little observation revealed her dire condition: a cotton rope had grown into her neck and was cutting off her circulation. Cecil had the rope cut off, and Daisy, now eight years old, has been his "best pal" since. Every morning Cecil says, "Come on, Daisy, let's go to work!" and they take off through the vineyards. Afterward, she rides in Cecil's truck or sits in the winery's trademark fire engine. She even flies with Cecil in his plane, to Chico, Los Angeles, Texas, and Colorado. She likes guests, and she endures the winery cats—even when they lie in her bed, forcing her to sleep outside. But no matter where she is or whom she's with, she's always got her eye on Cecil.

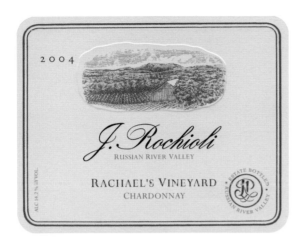

SAGE
J. ROCHIOLI VINEYARDS & WINERY

Sage, a twelve-year-old English springer spaniel, doesn't point or spring like his father did, or hunt ducks like his mother did. He has his own way. A loyal companion, he follows winery owner Tom Rochioli in the vineyard, in the winery, and throughout the picnic area, where he begs guests for their food. When he's tired, he stretches where he pleases—on his back, spread-eagle—or propped up halfway against a wall. Sage used to chase the resident winery cat, Sweet Pea, and everyone thought they'd be enemies for life. But one day, they were found sleeping together, warm and relaxed, and they've been good friends ever since.

2004
Trenton Estate Vineyard
Russian River Valley

Pinot Noir

Joseph Swan Vineyards

Grown, Produced and Bottled by Joseph Swan Vineyards
Forestville, California, Alcohol 14.5% by Volume

PAPPY
JOSEPH SWAN VINEYARDS

When a neighbor's daughter found Papillon on River Road, he was a lost dog with no home. Today, the twelve-year-old continental toy spaniel, known as "Pappy," is mischievous and quirky, stealing grain out of horses' buckets, smiling for cookies, and barking when people hug. But winery owners Rod and Lynn Berglund say he's also a social, affectionate companion. Most of the day he's at Rod's side, but he always runs to welcome guests the moment they arrive, living up to his reputation as the winery's doorbell. The winery cat, Cognac, used to be an enemy, but one day the Berglunds came home to find Pappy and Cognac nuzzling together as they slept, and they knew the war was over.

ROBBIE
KENDALL-JACKSON WINE ESTATES

Robbie, a four-year-old yellow Labrador retriever, is chief dog officer (CDO) for the winery, spending many of his weekdays at the office. Typically a low-key executive, things changed the moment he met O'Malley, a gorgeous golden retriever, at the winery proprietors' horse farm in Kentucky. Several months later, on Christmas Eve, O'Malley gave birth to eleven beautiful puppies, nine of whom reside in Sonoma County. All were quickly adopted by a Kendall-Jackson employee or family friend. The males are Bono, Gordie, Hurley, Marley, and Stanley, and the females are Eve, Maizy, Noëlle, and Siena. Proprietors Barbara Banke and Jess Jackson are thrilled to have this new generation of dogs working along with their CDO.

Noëlle (left) &
Gordie

Gordie (left) &
Robbie

Stanley (top) &
Noëlle

Marley (left) &
Eve

Eve (top) & Siena
Hurley (back)

KENDALL-JACKSON WINE ESTATES

Robbie loves to romp with his puppies during play dates at the winery. On 120 acres of pristine flower gardens, culinary gardens, wine sensory gardens, and a beautiful walnut grove, the dogs should be bounding from garden to grove, taking in all the wonderful scents. Instead, the puppies can't resist tumbling around with each other on the expansive lawn.

Bono (left) & Eve

Maizy

Frankie

FRANKIE & RUBY
MacMurray Ranch

Ruby

Ruby, a six-year-old yellow Labrador retriever, entertains onlookers when she swims in circles inside a wine barrel, gulping water as she gains speed. She also shares her food and water bowls with the winery's Bantham chickens. One winter, marketing director Roger Riccardi found a chick frozen in the feed bucket. Hopeful, he and Ruby ran to the car and Roger cranked the heat while Ruby cuddled with the chick. Today, Ruby and the rooster, Amy, remain the best of friends. Ruby is also friends with Frankie, a five-year-old Australian shepherd mix. "As long as Frankie can get out on a truck or a hike, he's happy," says spokesperson Kate MacMurray. A "wonderful companion," he hikes with Kate in the vineyards and swims in Porter Creek and the Russian River. He also converses with squirrels in an oak tree and barks at the marauding wild hogs from a distance. When it's time to relax, Frankie finds the window seat in the historic ranch's den, stretches out, and basks in the sun.

BRUTUS, JASMINE & PEPPER
MOSHIN VINEYARDS

Pepper (front),
Brutus & Jasmine

Pepper (left),
Brutus & Jasmine

In the mornings, Brutus and Jasmine, the nine-year-old Rhodesian ridgebacks, saunter in the vineyard beside Pepper, the six-year-old mutt of unknown origin, sniffing for new animal scents. In the evenings, as the fog rolls in from the Russian River, they're back in the vineyards, living the ideal life that Indy, the winery's first Rhodesian ridgeback, lived for many years. Brutus, a sweet and loving dog, stays away from trouble, but Jasmine is more exploratory. One day Jasmine chased a huge wild boar to the fence, and vice president Janet Moshin shook with fear, knowing the boar would win any fight. Suddenly, the hairy, smelly beast reared its tusks and snorted, and Jasmine ran humbly back to Janet, her tail between her legs. Pepper first came to Janet as a scared, bony puppy, hiding under Janet's car during an ice storm. In days, he fit in perfectly with the Moshin family, eating well and rushing through the rows chasing rabbits.

GAZER
MUELLER WINERY

Lucky Starr Gazer, a nine-year-old vizsla, has high energy outside and inside. In the outdoors, Gazer points to anything that moves, including butterflies, and when he gets a whiff of a cat, he takes off running until he's out of sight, forcing winery owners Lori and Bob Mueller to keep him on a leash. Indoors, he's an active playmate for the Muellers' daughter, Emily, and he's respectful of Catso, the house cat, who feels free to roam the house without worry. In the mornings, Bob and Lori appreciate Gazer's ability to bring them a half cup of coffee without any spills. Then, just as the Muellers settle in with their coffee, Gazer will jump into their laps for affection, not realizing that at sixty pounds, he can never be a lapdog.

PHILIP STALEY

2005
Viognier
Russian River Valley

ALC. 14.2% BY VOL.

MURPHY
PHILIP STALEY VINEYARDS & WINERY

Murphy, a seven-year-old golden retriever, came to winery owner Philip Staley as a rebellious eighteen-month-old. Raised by an elderly woman who was not active enough to take care of her, Murphy had gotten too little attention and direction. Wasting no time, Philip hired a dog trainer—and former horse whisperer—and today Murphy is beautifully obedient, following Philip wherever he goes. As a bonus, her easygoing affection extends to all people and other dogs. In the vineyard, as Philip oversees the grape growing for his small lots of wine, Murphy runs freely through the rows—and gladly runs back to Philip at the first call.

ESTANCIA, ZACKARY & DIEGO
PORTER CREEK VINEYARDS

ESTATE BOTTLED

PORTER CREEK

2004
RUSSIAN RIVER VALLEY
PINOT NOIR
Fiona Hill Vineyard

Zackary

Estancia

Estancia, a ten-year-old Jack Russell terrier/fox terrier/whippet mix, and Zackary, a nine-year-old German shepherd/Akita mix, are at the winery every day, rain or shine. In the mornings they run up and down the vineyards, sniffing deeply, and then the staff calls them into the tasting room for hours of relaxation and customer appreciation. Diego, a one-year-old Great Pyrenees, will one day be a great watchdog. For now, though, he's still chewing on the vines and on UPS packages left on winery owner George Davis's front porch. Remarkably unsubtle, he leaves giant paw prints on the walls of his home and the tasting room. When he gets tired of decorating the walls, he naps in his special doghouse, an oversized wine barrel, and excitedly wakes up to greet customers.

Diego

BUSTER
RABBIT RIDGE VINEYARDS & WINERY

Three years ago, warehouse manager and hospitality coordinator Craig Wisdom arrived at a Ukiah shelter in search of a dog. In minutes, Buster—a friendly black Labrador retriever/McNab mix—was the pick. Now four years old, Buster is glad to see everyone. He's a friend to cats, he howls with happiness when he plays with dogs, and he runs to the parking lot to see visitors. He loves games, and he'll nip at a person's pant legs to entice a chase. A former escape artist, Buster used to sneak out of the Wisdoms' backyard, and no one could figure out how he got over the tall fence. One day he was caught in the act, walking silently along the narrow edge of the above-ground pool, and Craig had to put up a new barrier. These days Buster has no need to escape—he follows Craig everywhere at work, prompting employees to call him "Shadow."

KIRI TE KANAWA
RUSSIAN HILL ESTATE WINERY

Kiri Te Kanawa, an eight-year-old Australian shepherd, was named after the famous opera singer. Only later did winemaker Patrick Melley discover that the two Kiris share the same birthday. True to her namesake, the shepherd is a "diva to the extreme," says Patrick. Most blatantly, whenever a vineyard worker pushes a wheelbarrow through the vineyard, Kiri jumps inside for a ride. One day she demanded more of a show, riding in the most conspicuous part of the tractor—out front, "like a hood ornament!" Patrick exclaims. When she's not riding in high style, she's chasing any bird that alights on the vines or swimming the length of the nearby irrigation ponds. Always refreshed and energetic, she's happy to lead all visitors to the winery.

Oscar (front) &
Bogart

OSCAR
TAFT STREET WINERY

It must be hard to be a dog in a land full of cats, or so it must seem to Oscar, a four-month-old black Labrador retriever/boxer mix. In his young life, he's already been forced to deal with countless feral cats roaming the vineyards, thanks to winery partner Susan Martini. Susan regularly traps new cats, takes them to a Sonoma shelter for spaying and neutering, and brings them home to the winery. On any given day, five cats stop by her big cat bowl for a meal. And while Oscar has no trouble scaring them away when he's in the mood, he's found nothing but trouble with Finnegan, Susan's brave, yellow domestic cat. Even when Oscar won't stop barking, Finnegan stands his ground, occasionally swatting at Oscar's nose for effect. Frustrated, Oscar pulls the wheels off the office chairs and chews them, or he finds comfort sleeping next to Susan's desk at the winery. Sometimes his friend Bogart, a friendly boxer from Radio-Coteau Winery, shows up to play, and Oscar can forget all about the cats.

Oscar (front) &
Bogart

HANK WILLIAMS JR. & LOLA
TOAD HOLLOW VINEYARDS

Hank

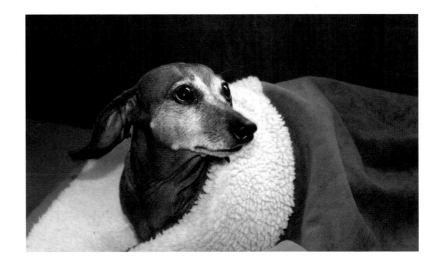

For the most part, Hank Williams Junior, a nine-year-old dachshund, enjoys a relaxing life with winery owners Todd and Frankie Williams. Between photo shoots for the Toad Hollow wine labels, Hank eats sweet Pinot Noir grapes, sleeps draped around Todd's neck while Todd sits in his high-back desk chair, and naps some more under his favorite sleeping bag. But then Lola, a two-year-old Jack Russell terrier, walks in with her stylish pink coat. Energized by the walks she takes with Julie Maas, consumer direct manager, Lola harasses Hank whenever she can, nudging him when he's resting peacefully under the sleeping bag. Though the two dogs are rarely in sync, they each bring cheer to the winery. Lola entertains everyone with her vivacity, and Hank radiates joy. "A winery dog brings happiness to the winery," Todd says. "While I can be grumpy sometimes, when I am walking Hank I am happy."

Lola

119

Sonoma Carneros

Homewood Winery

Larson Family Winery

Robledo Family Winery

Roche Carneros Estate Winery

Sonoma Coast

Flowers Vineyard & Winery

Gallo Family Vineyards

Keller Estate Winery

Peaches

BEAU, PEACHES & LILY
HOMEWOOD WINERY

Beau Regard, a nine-year-old chocolate Labrador retriever, is most at home among throngs of people, inside the tasting room or outside by the picnic tables. Off site, Samantha Williams, tasting room manager, takes athletic Beau to Stinson Beach for body surfing and to the mountains for full-moon snowshoeing. Peaches, a one-year-old Weimaraner mix, was found on a peach farm. When tasting room employee Roshinee Punian adopted her, she was "nine pounds of bones" and recovering from parvo. Today, at sixty-five pounds, she wiggles her backside when she's excited and licks Beau's face whenever he allows it. Lily, a three-month-old teacup Chihuahua, is so tiny that she's only in the tasting room, playing with Beau, when the crowds let up. "She's still learning her social graces," says Heather Seely, the assistant tasting room manager. Out in the vineyard, she tugs on the canes in the ground and proudly brings sticks to Heather.

Lily

Beau

Max (top) &
Sunny

Sunny

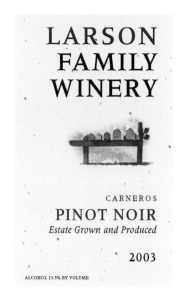

LARSON
FAMILY
WINERY

CARNEROS
PINOT NOIR
Estate Grown and Produced

2003

ALCOHOL 13.5% BY VOLUME

RUFF, MAX & SUNNY
LARSON FAMILY WINERY

Ruff

"It takes a lot of dog to make good wine," say winery owners Tom and Becky Larson. On the former Sonoma County rodeo grounds and racetrack, in the company of a llama and a sheep, three dogs do their part. The Texas-born black Labrador retriever, Ruff Doyle, is 19 years old. In his younger days, he often ran away with the poodle down the road, visiting the local café or jumping into the creek backside first. These days, he rests companionably under Becky's desk. Max, an eight-year-old Labrador retriever/chow mix, failed obedience school three times. Giving up, the Larsons let Max find his own routine. Most days he rides on top of the vineyard workers' truck, sleeping as they work and staying on top as they slowly drive back to the winery. Sunny, a two-year-old yellow Labrador retriever, can often entice Max to run with him to the creek and chase sticks. At night, Ruff, Max, and Sunny sleep at the winery, loyally protecting their home.

Zorro

ZORRO & MAGNUM
ROBLEDO FAMILY WINERY

Magnum

Zorro, an eight-year-old Chihuahua, loves to socialize and to sleep. He arrives at the tasting room every day with vineyard manager Everardo Robledo, running up to his adoring fans, some of whom visit the winery just to see him. He used to sleep with the winery's indulgent German shepherd, Remy. One day, as he slept beneath Remy's saddle, a visitor could see only Remy's oddly raised back and remarked, "How sad, your dog has a gigantic tumor." Instantly, Zorro reared his little head and got everyone laughing. These days Zorro sleeps on the back of Magnum, a three-year-old yellow Labrador retriever. Cellarmaster Francisco Robledo says that Magnum is an admirable worker, chasing jackrabbits and digging for gophers every day. But no matter how much success he has on the hunt, Magnum attracts the most attention during his naps with Zorro, the tiny winery celebrity.

AMBER & DRAKE
ROCHE CARNEROS ESTATE WINERY

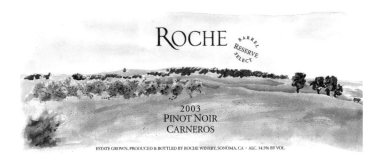

Drake

Amber

Amber, a twelve-year-old Labrador retriever mix, is fiercely devoted to winemaker Michael Carr. She follows him to the lab and the tanks, where drips of Pinot Noir decorate her beautiful white coat with purple lines and spots. If she loses sight of him, she runs around desperately, and winery employees help reunite Amber with her best friend. Drake, a mellow eleven-year-old black Labrador retriever, has a tail that never stops wagging. Even when he was under anesthesia—completely out—to get a foxtail removed from his ear, Drake's tail slowly and steadily wagged. General manager Brendan Roche says that while Drake's dream is to live indoors and eat leftovers, he can't resist a trip to the irrigation lake. Drake swims and retrieves sticks, bringing them back for sumptuous chewing, and sometimes Amber is there, too, sloshing in the mud, chasing frogs, and flirting with Drake.

Maggie

MAGGIE, SIMBA & DACITE
FLOWERS VINEYARD & WINERY

2004

FLOWERS
Sonoma Coast

PINOT NOIR
SONOMA COAST

*Simba (left) &
Maggie*

Dacite

"It's nice to see a wagging tail in the heat of work," says winery president Tom Hinde. "It calms the nerves." Simba, Maggie, and Dacite are the three dogs who wag their tails at Flowers. Simba, a twelve-year-old "full-blown mutt," was a shy rescue puppy, says associate winemaker Darrin Low. Today, however, he is unabashedly affectionate with women when he's not distracted by a rabbit nibbling on the vines. Maggie, a five-year-old black Labrador retriever, took to riding the forklift immediately, says general manager Jesse Tidwell. In the office, she snoops in the kitchen for treats and plays with the toys Jesse keeps under his desk. Dacite, a four-year-old Australian stumpy tail cattle dog, walks on two legs waiting for winemaker Ross Cobb to wake up in the morning. At the winery, she takes frequent dips in the nearby pond and runs around with Simba and Maggie.

DOT
GALLO FAMILY VINEYARDS

Five years ago, vineyard manager Dennis Devitt found a skinny, weak Dalmatian puppy. Today Dot is a healthy runner and obedient companion. Every morning, Dot hops in the truck and Dennis drives to a vineyard. Full of excitement, she flies through the rows, never losing sight of the truck and always listening for Dennis's call. Even when she's pursuing a rabbit alongside newly planted vines, she'll stop dead in her tracks when Dennis calls and run to his side. When she's not running, she's a companion to all who stop by the Gallo Family Vineyards Laguna Ranch office. On at least three occasions, Dot has run happily up to what she seems to think is a black-and-white cat. Dennis has tried, yet failed, to convince her that the playmate is actually a skunk. Fortunately, the patient skunk has not exacted revenge for Dot's misidentification.

Shadow

134

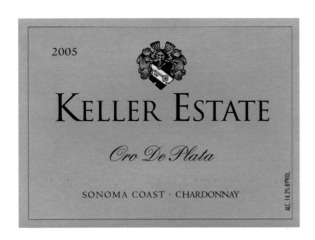

MARA & SHADOW
KELLER ESTATE WINERY

Mara

Shadow, a nine-year-old German shepherd, has found a best friend in Mara, a four-year-old Rhodesian ridgeback. Together they run all day through Keller Estate's 600 acres of Pinot Noir and Chardonnay vines. Shadow impresses everyone with her graceful gait as she glides silently through the rows in pursuit of rabbits. Mara, a true athlete, is the faster runner, using all her muscle to break her own records for speed. When it's time for rest, snacks, and affection, they know they can count on the vineyard workers, who are happy to see them settle down for a while. At home, they stay close to general manager Ana Keller. Mara, unaware of her own size, usually finds her way to Ana's lap.

Sonoma Valley

B.R. Cohn Winery

David Noyes Wines

Gundlach Bundschu Winery

Kaz Vineyard & Winery

Kunde Estate Winery & Vineyards

Landmark Vineyards

Moondance Cellars/The Friendly Dog Winery

Petroni Vineyards

Sebastiani Vineyards & Winery

St. Francis Winery

The Wine Room

Sonoma Mountain

Benziger Family Winery

Charles Creek Vineyard

MOOSE
B.R. COHN WINERY

When winery owner Bruce Cohn's yellow Labrador retriever escaped and mated with one of his prized English bulldogs, a star was born. Weighing in at 93 pounds, the eight-year-old Moose has all the trappings of celebrity. He has his own line of dog biscuits, a line of T-shirts, and his own wine, a bestselling blend called Moose's Red. His label spells out his ambitious mission to "eat well, be loved, get petted, and sleep a lot." And as events manager Paula Horosco reveals, Moose can't get enough of the spotlight. In the tasting room, he calls attention to himself with his Buddha pose, exposing his big belly while seated on his hind legs. Then, with all eyes on him, he rolls onto his back with his legs sprawled in the air, displaying a shocking pose meriting an "R" rating. When the fans calm down, he indulges his youngest admirers by letting them climb all over him. At times the world is too much for him, so he jumps in the truck for a ride, taking in the view of the vineyards that make his lavish lifestyle possible.

ALLIE
David Noyes Wines

Allie, a sixteen-year-old sheltie mix with long, wavy hair, has been aging gracefully. Winemaker David Noyes says Allie is a "wonderful receptionist" at his home when he and Grace Noyes serve David's wine at dinner parties. In the vineyards, when David typically spends five hours a day evaluating the vines, Allie is great company, chasing rabbits and squirrels yet spending most of her time beside David. After the days in the field, she enjoys excellent home care. Grace, a chiropractor, carefully adjusts Allie's shoulder and back. Isabelle Ansell, Grace's daughter and a massage therapist for people, stops by to massage her favorite canine client. Sensitive to people in pain, Allie is the perfect cure, sitting beside them and providing gentle comfort.

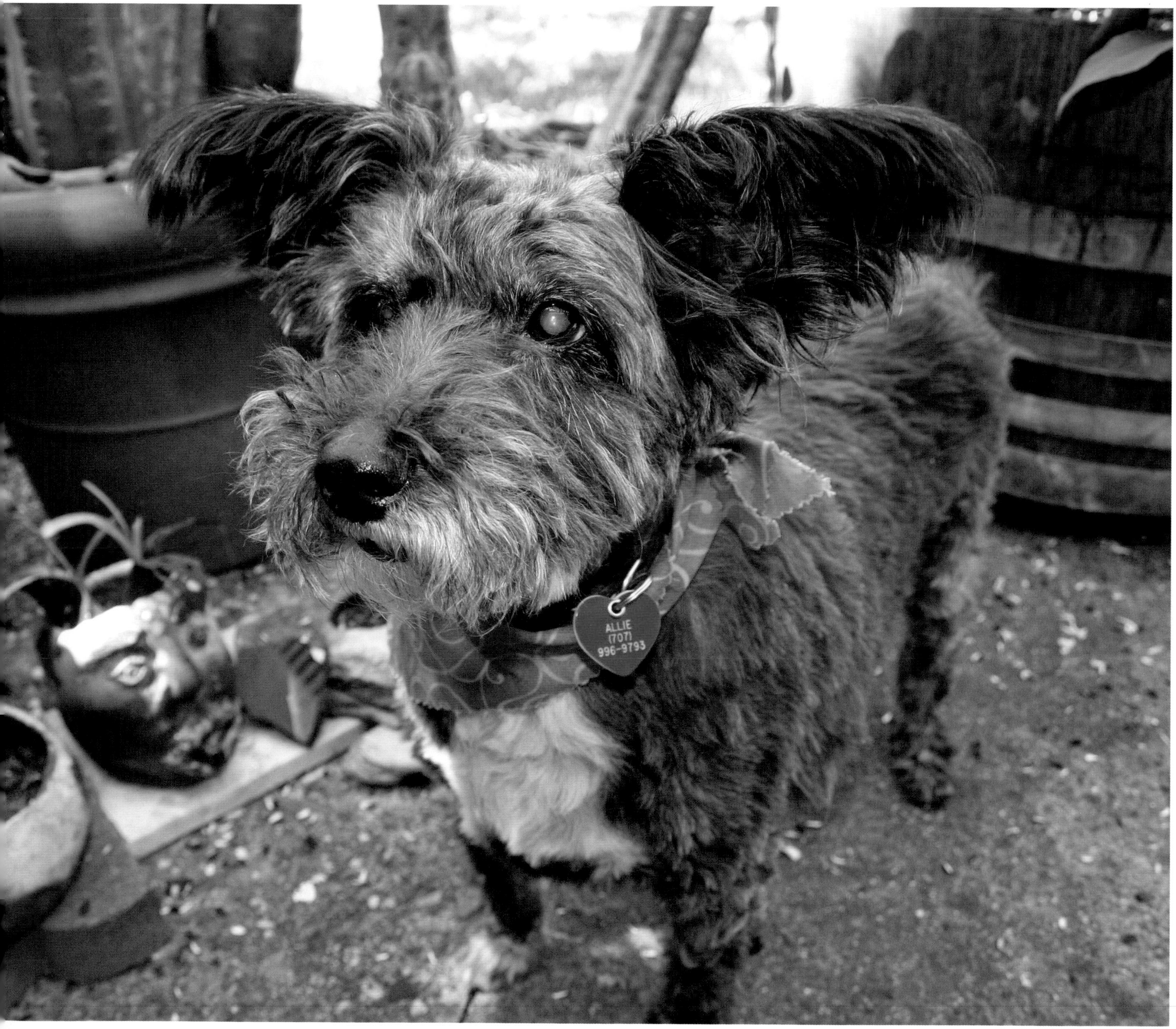
ALLIE
(707)
996-9793

ROSIE
GUNDLACH BUNDSCHU WINERY

Rosie, a nine-year-old yellow Labrador retriever, accompanies winery owner Jim Bundschu each day, riding in the truck or walking beside him for hours as he inspects the vines. And though she's content to be with Jim all day, she occasionally runs to get petted by the welcoming vineyard workers. Unfortunately for the Bundschus, baths are not to Rosie's liking—she prefers to roll in the dirt. Fortunately, she also likes to swim briskly in the clear ponds. When Jim brings her along to duck hunts, she sometimes gets so excited that she jumps wildly on all four feet and scares away the ducks. At home she's calm, cooling down in Nancy's large beds of pink lilies and emerging instantly—her tail wagging—whenever Jim and Nancy walk by.

Max & Maude

Chocolate

MAX, MAUDE, CHOCOLATE & CARTUCHO
GUNDLACH BUNDSCHU WINERY

"Contact with domestic pets adds a lot to the general environment at a winery," says vineyard manager Michael Raymor. He brings the two German shepherds, eighteen-year-old Max and ten-year-old Maude, to chase deer and rabbits from the vines and socialize with the vineyard workers. The workers also love and care for Chocolate, a five-year-old chocolate Labrador retriever, and Cartucho, a one-year-old Chihuahua mix. Though the two younger dogs are both good company in the field, the quick Cartucho is an antagonist, willing to challenge any big dog. Chocolate, as his name suggests, is sweet, and he refuses to take the funny Cartucho's challenge. All four dogs form a happy social group and share a fascination with motor vehicles. "They're always looking for a ride," Michael says.

Cartucho

COTI
KAZ VINEYARD & WINERY

Richard Kasmier, or "Kaz," is free-spirited and fun, and his winemaking philosophy is reflected in his favorite expressions, "Do it how you like it" and "There's no harm in experimenting." So it's no surprise that his daughter, Kristin Kasmier (the winery's "whip cracker"), brought Coti to the family business. Affectionately known as "Monster," the four-year-old bull terrier/Jack Russell terrier mix got his start in San Diego, first as a shelter dog and then, at Kristin's side, as a wild dog, swimming and chasing surfers in the ocean. In the vineyard in Sonoma, Coti chases and eats bees with zeal. Anyone who wants a demonstration of his skill and high energy need only throw a tennis ball his way. Coti will catch it—midair—no matter how often it's thrown. His perpetual enthusiasm and fun-loving attitude make him a perfect fit at Kaz.

Riley (left) &
Jasper

RILEY & JASPER
KUNDE ESTATE WINERY & VINEYARDS

veryone who knows Labrador retrievers is aware of their first love: food. But as much as Jasper (age six) and Riley (age two) adore eating, their favorite thing to do is to run freely at the estate. When winery owners Jeff and Roberta Kunde open their car doors, the black and yellow Labs race to the pond and splash wildly beneath the fountain. Nearby customers—whether they're on their way to the tasting room or waiting for a cave tour—become entranced by the show, and it's not unusual to see thirty people laughing at the happy dogs. Jasper and Riley are great companions for the Kunde family, accompanying them during hikes and horseback riding on the property. "The dogs are good mascots," says Jeff, "and they give the winery a down-home feel."

Riley (left) &
Jasper

SPANKY
LANDMARK VINEYARDS

Spanky, a fourteen-year-old rough-coated Jack Russell terrier, was named after one of the Little Rascals. One day he went missing and no one could find him. From a distance, winery owners Mike and Mary Colhoun spotted an ear sticking out of a garbage can and walked over to find him munching with gusto on a burrito. When he's not scrounging for food, he's retrieving golf balls for Mike or gathering wine bungs for his own special collection. If the Colhouns don't stop him, he can pile up 35 bungs and still be looking for more. He loves parties, especially the Colhouns' New Year's Eve gala, when he's dressed in a tuxedo. As anyone could guess, Spanky keeps the energy high until long past midnight.

BINGO & GHOST
MOONDANCE CELLARS/
THE FRIENDLY DOG WINERY

THE FRIENDLY DOG WINERY

BINGO

2003
14021 in dog years
Napa Valley
Zinfandel

ALC 13.4% BY VOL

Ghost

Bingo

"They are like a flock of birds," says Priscilla Cohen, referring to the winery's two Australian shepherds, both six years old. Usually inseparable, Bingo and Ghost come and go together, greeting Priscilla and David Cohen's customers at the winery and chasing gophers in the vineyards, each doing a fine job of trenching the property. Sometimes Bingo leaves the gophers alone to indulge his strange desire to bury left-handed gloves (never the right) in his carefully sculpted holes. As the two shepherds bury and dig, the winery's horses—Jester, Minnie, and Seco—throw their manes up to taunt the dogs. Guided by instinct, Bingo and Ghost rush to herd them, though the horses are always safely enclosed by a strong gate.

Ghost (left) &
Bingo

PETRONI

Poggio Alla Pietra
Estate Grown

2 0 0 3

EMMA & BELLA
PETRONI VINEYARDS

Bella

According to everyone at Petroni Vineyards, Emma, an eighteen-year-old Labrador retriever/Rhodesian ridgeback mix, is president. Bella, an eight-year-old Labrador retriever/Akita mix, is vice president. Together, say winery owners Lorenzo and Maria Elena Petroni, they keep the winery running efficiently. Emma loves to be part of the action, sitting on the forklift and interacting with employees who operate the heavy machinery. Bella, who is afraid of the forklift, is better suited for chasing deer and rabbits from the vines. Thanks to a shared love of food, they both charm guests at lavish culinary events, enjoying their share of Tuscan cuisine—olives, breadsticks, prosciutto, and freshly baked bread. When their bellies are full, they like to nap in the shade of the olive grove or on the cool cellar floor.

Emma

Rubee (top) &
Emmy Lou

156

SEBASTIANI
FAMILY OWNED SINCE 1904
2003

ALC. 13.5% BY VOL.

CABERNET SAUVIGNON
SONOMA COUNTY

B, RUBEE & EMMY LOU
SEBASTIANI VINEYARDS & WINERY

B

At Sebastiani, visiting dogs don't have to stay in their cars—the winery has posts, leashes, and bowls of water waiting. And in the summer, the winery's Canine Festival features bobbing for hot dogs and a dog fashion show. B, Rubee, and Emmy Lou are the lucky dogs who play at Sebastiani every day. B, a twelve-year-old yellow Labrador retriever, likes people more than food. Adopted from a shelter only a year ago by chief operating officer Emma Swain, B prefers nothing more than to hang out with Emma in the office. Rubee, a nine-year-old Boston terrier, must have royal blood because people all over the winery refer to her as "the queen." Mary Ann Sebastiani Cuneo, winery president and chief executive officer, says that Rubee loves to socialize with her many subjects. Emmy Lou, a five-year-old English black Labrador retriever, spends her days with Kelly Conrad, director of marketing. Emmy Lou's powerful nose and sharp timing mean that any food that is momentarily forgotten suddenly disappears. Despite the enthusiasm that these dogs bring, Meredith Crotty, marketing coordinator, says, "Dogs are really a calming force at the winery." Of course, Sebastiani intends to keep it that way.

Abby

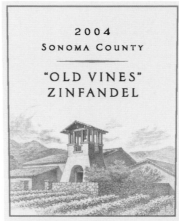

2004
SONOMA COUNTY

"OLD VINES"
ZINFANDEL

WINSTON & ABBY
ST. FRANCIS WINERY

"Winston is the picture-perfect definition of absurdity," says Lauren Mackey, daughter of winemaker Thomas Mackey. And as Thomas confirms, Winston, a five-year-old bassett hound, is quirky. Terrified of water in all forms, he doesn't know how to howl, and he would rather socialize with people than other dogs. During the winery's annual blessing of the animals, however, many of Winston's siblings—up to fifteen of them—reunite with him for some fun. New on the scene is ten-month-old Abby, a playful Greater Swiss Mountain dog. At home with chief financial officer Robert Aldridge, Abby likes to grab a roll of toilet paper and run through the house. At work, she gallops from person to person, lying down to sleep for a few minutes and then getting up to gallop to more people. Occasionally, she'll take a break from the crowd to sip from one of the winery's famous fountains.

Winston (left) &
Abby

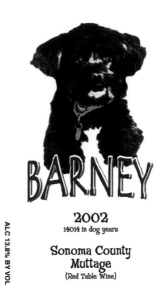

BARNEY

2002
14014 in dog years

Sonoma County
Muttage
(Red Table Wine)

ALC 13.8% BY VOL

BARNEY
THE WINE ROOM

Barney, a three-year-old poodle/terrier mix, is a regular at The Wine Room, a wine cooperative. Wine club members Mary Jo and Dick Kulp adopted the unknown Barney from the Animal Rescue Foundation, and today he has his own label, Barney's Blend, which is the first wine a customer sees upon entering. Sociable and playful, Barney works the crowd when he arrives and shows off his favorite toy, a plastic hamburger, which he holds under his foot in case someone is unsure about its ownership. Another toy is a stuffed monkey that Barney uses to push the hamburger across the room. Then, in a move designed to prove, once again, who owns his favorite toy, Barney runs to the magnificent hamburger, placing his paw on top and scanning the room of laughing customers.

Goober

SIERRA & GOOBER
BENZIGER FAMILY WINERY

A long time part of the Benziger Family Winery, Sierra is a beloved fourteen-year-old yellow Labrador retriever. In her younger days, she chased pheasants, but today she strolls with Jeanne Reiser, the winery's administration manager, through the biodynamic vineyards among the beautiful gardens and fountains. Thirteen-year-old Goober, a chocolate Labrador retriever, is similarly calm but is also what winery owner Chris Benziger calls "an independent old man." In his younger days, Goober rode on the tram during vineyard tours, quiet and content to feel the breeze on his face. Today, when he's not tipping over garbage cans to search for scraps, he's meandering through the office and grounds to be sure the younger dogs are doing their jobs.

RUSTY, FANCY & JAKE
BENZIGER FAMILY WINERY

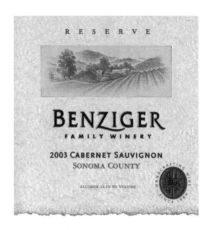

Rusty

Fancy

Rusty, a seven-year-old cocker spaniel, came to the winery as a lovable but overweight dog. Today, graphic artist Paulette Nolan has helped him achieve a healthy weight through diet and exercise, though he spends much of the day going from office to office looking for handouts. Five-year-old Fancy, an Australian shepherd, loves to spend her days with Bart Hansen, the cellarmaster. With her positive attitude, she brings happiness to the office and enjoys a good belly rub any time of day. Three-year-old Jake, a yellow Labrador retriever and Fancy's favorite canine pal, is an accomplished swimmer who would chase sticks all day if someone would keep throwing them. When he jumps into the Jeep with Mark Burningham, vice president of production, and Tracy Burningham, business operations manager, Jake gets so excited that he rolls down his own window and hangs his head out in anticipation of the ride.

Jake

Maddy

RUBY & FOWL WEATHER MADNESS

CHARLES CREEK VINEYARD

Ruby

The Brinton family loves the Charles Creek vineyard, which they own, and loves duck hunting almost as much. Whenever possible, Bill hunts with two talented black Labrador retrievers, twelve-year-old Ruby and four-year-old Fowl Weather Madness ("Maddy" to most), taking them in the bow of his boat to their destinations. Ruby, who is semi-retired from the avid duck chasing, usually lies in the blind with Bill, keeping him company. Maddy, however, is an AKC-certified senior hunter, impressing Bill with her instant recognition of hand signals and swift retrievals. To keep them in shape between hunts, Gerry Brinton tosses sticks and balls far out into the vineyard, amazed that they never seem to grow tired. At harvest, the duo helps Bill with a major decision. "They know when the grapes are ready for picking," he says. "When the sugar and taste are almost right, they gobble them up."

WINERY LISTING

A. Rafanelli Winery
4685 W. Dry Creek Road, Healdsburg, CA 95448
(707) 433-1385
www.arafanelliwinery.com
Tasting by appointment

Alexander Valley Vineyards
8644 Highway 128, Healdsburg, CA 95448
(707) 433-7209 or (800) 888-7209
www.avvwine.com
avv@avvwine.com
Tasting, 10-5 Daily

Atascadero Creek Winery
PO Box 691, Graton, CA 95444
(707) 824-8204
www.atascaderocreek.com
info@atascaderocreek.com
Tasting by appointment

Arista Winery
7015 Westside Road, Healdsburg, CA 95448
(707) 473-0606
www.aristawinery.com
info@aristawinery.com
Tasting, 11-5 Thu-Mon, Tues & Wed by appointment

Armida Winery
2201 Westside Road, Healdsburg, CA 95448
(707) 433-2222
www.armida.com
info@armida.com
Tasting, 11-5 Daily
Tours by appointment

Bella Vineyards & Wine Caves
9711 W. Dry Creek Road, Healdsburg, CA 95448
(866) 57-BELLA (572- 3552)
www.bellawinery.com
info@bellawinery.com
Tasting, 11-4:30 Daily

Benziger Family Winery
1883 London Ranch Road, Glen Ellen, CA 95442
(888) 490-2739
www.benziger.com
greatwine@benziger.com
Tasting, 10-5 Daily
Tours offered daily

B.R. Cohn Winery
15000 Sonoma Highway, Glen Ellen, CA 95442
(800) 330-4064
www.brcohn.com
info@brcohn.com
Tasting, 10-5 Daily

Camellia Cellars
57 Front Street, Healdsburg, CA 95448
(707) 433-1290 or (888) 404-WINE
www.camelliacellars.com
Tasting, 11-6 Daily

Carol Shelton Wines
(707) 575-3441
www.carolshelton.com
zin@carolshelton.com

Charles Creek Vineyard
Tasting Room & Gallery:
483 First Street West, Sonoma, CA 95476
(707) 935-3848
www.charlescreek.com
tastewine@charlescreek.com
Tasting, 11-6 Daily

Chateau Felice
Tasting Room:
223 Center Street, Healdsburg, CA 95448
(707) 431-9010
www.chateaufelice.com
samantha@chateaufelice.com
Tasting, 10-5 Daily

Christopher Creek Winery
641 Limerick Lane, Healdsburg, CA 95448
(707) 433-2001
www.christophercreek.com
info@christophercreek.com
Tasting, 11-5 Daily, or appointment

Clos du Bois
19410 Geyserville Avenue, Geyserville, CA 95441
(707) 857-3100 or (800) 222-3189
www.closdubois.com
tastingroom@closdubois.com
Tasting, 10-4:30 Daily

Collier Falls Vineyard
9931 W. Dry Creek Road, Healdsburg, CA 95448
(707) 433-7373
www.collierfalls.com
wine@collierfalls.com
Tasting at Family Wineries Tasting Room
10:30-4:30 Daily
4791 Dry Creek Road., Healdsburg, CA 95448
(888) 433-6555
www.familywines.com

David Noyes Wines
620 Oman Springs Circle, Sonoma, CA 95476
(707) 935-7741
www.davidnoyeswines.com
dgnoyes@sbcglobal.net

Davis Bynum Winery
8075 Westside Road, Healdsburg, CA 95448
(707) 433-5852 or (800) 826-1073
www.davisbynum.com
celeste@davisbynum.com
Tasting, 10-5 Daily

De La Montanya Winery & Vineyards
999 Foreman Lane, Healdsburg, CA 95448
(707) 433-3711
www.dlmwine.com
dennis@dlmwine.com
Tasting, 11-4:30 Sat-Sun, or by appointment

Dehlinger Winery
4101 Vine Hill Road, Sebastopol, CA 95472
(707) 823-2378
www.dehlingerwinery.com

Dry Creek Vineyard
3770 Lambert Bridge Road, Healdsburg, CA 95448
(707) 433-1000 or (800) 864-9463
www.drycreekvineyard.com
dcv@drycreekvineyard.com
Tasting, 10:30–4:30 Daily

F. Teldeschi Winery
3555 Dry Creek Road, Healdsburg, CA 95448
(707) 433-6626
www.teldeschi.com
dteldeschi@neteze.com
Tasting, 12-5 Daily, or by appointment

Flowers Vineyard & Winery
28500 Seaview Road, Cazadero, CA 95421
(707) 847-3661
www.flowerswinery.com
info@flowerswinery.com

Forchini Vineyards & Winery
5141 Dry Creek Road, Healdsburg, CA 95448
(707) 431-8886
www.forchini.com
wine@forchini.com
Tasting, 11-4 Fri–Sun, or by appointment

Frick Winery
23072 Walling Road, Geyserville, CA 95441
(707) 857-1980
www.frickwinery.com
frick@frickwinery.com
Tasting, 12-4:30 Sat-Sun

Fritz Winery
24691 Dutcher Creek Road, Cloverdale, CA 95425
(707) 894-3389
www.fritzwinery.com
info@fritzwinery.com
Tasting, 10:30–4:30 Daily

Gallo Family Vineyards
3387 Dry Creek Road, Healdsburg, CA 95448
www.gallofamilyvineyards.com
Tasting available at
Gallo Family Tasting Room
320 Center Street, Healdsburg, CA 95448
(707) 433-2458
tours@gallosonoma.com
Tasting, 10-6 Daily

Gundlach Bundschu Winery
2000 Denmark Street, Sonoma, CA 95476
(707) 939-3015
www.gunbun.com
info@gunbun.com
Tasting, 11-4:30 Daily

Hart's Desire Wines
25094 Asti Road, Cloverdale, CA 95425
(707) 579-1687
www.hartsdesirewines.com
john@hartsdesirewines.com
Tasting by appointment

Harvest Moon Estate & Winery
2192 Olivet Road, Santa Rosa, CA 95401
(707) 573-8711
www.harvestmoonwinery.com
info@harvestmoonwinery.com
Tasting, 10:30–4:30 Daily

Hook & Ladder Vineyards and Winery
2134 Olivet Road, Santa Rosa, CA 95401
(707) 526-2255
www.hookandladderwinery.com
info@hookandladderwinery.com
Tasting, 10-4:30 Daily

Homewood Winery
23120 Burndale Road, Sonoma, CA 95476
(707) 996-6353
www.homewoodwinery.com
Tasting, 10–4 Daily, or by appointment

Johnson's Alexander Valley Wines
8333 Highway 128, Healdsburg, CA 95448
(707) 433-2319
winery@johnsonwines.com
Tasting, 10-5 Daily

Joseph Swan Vineyards
2916 Laguna Road, Forestville, CA 95436
(707) 573-3747
www.swanwinery.com
rod@swanwinery.com
Tasting, 11–4:30 Sat & Sun, or by appointment Mon & Fri

Kaz Vineyard & Winery
233 Adobe Canyon Road, Kenwood, CA 95452
(877) 833-2536
www.kazwinery.com
Tasting, 1–5 Fri–Mon, or by appointment

Keller Estate Winery
5875 Lakeville Hwy, Petaluma, CA 94954
(707) 765-2117
www.kellerestate.com
Tasting by appointment

Kendall-Jackson Wine Estates
5007 Fulton Road, Fulton, CA 95439
(866) 287-9818 or (707) 571-8100
www.kj.com
Tasting, 10–5 Daily

Kendall-Jackson Healdsburg Tasting Room
337 Healdsburg Avenue, Healdsburg, CA 95448
(707) 433-7102
Tasting, 10-5 Daily

Kunde Estate Winery & Vineyards
9825 Sonoma Highway, Kenwood, CA 95452
(707) 833-5501
www.kunde.com
wineinfo@kunde.com
Tasting, 10:30–4:30 Daily

Landmark Vineyards
101 Adobe Canyon Road, Kenwood, CA 95452
(707) 833-0053
www.landmarkwine.com
info@landmarkwine.com
Tasting, 10:30-4:30 Daily

Larson Family Winery
23355 Millerick Road, Sonoma, CA 95476
(707) 938-3031
www.larsonfamilywinery.com
backy@larsonfamilywinery.com
Tasting, 10-5 Daily

MacMurray Ranch
(888) 668-7729
www.macmurrayranch.com

Mauritson Wines
2859 Dry Creek Road, Healdsburg, CA 95448
(707) 431-0804
www.mauritsonwines.com
info@mauritsonwines.com
Tasting, 10-5 Daily

Meeker Vineyard
21035 Geyserville Avenue, Geyserville, CA 95441
(707) 431-2148
www.meekerwine.com
eddie@meekerwine.com
Tasting, 10:30-6 Mon-Sat, 12-5 Sun

Michel-Schlumberger Wine Estate
4155 Wine Creek Road, Healdsburg, CA 95448
(707) 433-7427 or (800) 447-3060
www.michelschlumberger.com
Tasting by appointment only, 11:00 or 2:00 Daily

Mill Creek Vineyards & Winery
1401 Westside Road, Healdsburg, CA 95448
(707) 431-2121
www.mcvonline.com
tr@millcreekwinery.com
Tasting, 10-5 Daily

Moondance Cellars/ The Friendly Dog Winery
(707) 823-0880
www.moondancecellars.com
info@moondancecellars.com
Tasting at The Wine Room
9575 Sonoma Highway, Kenwood, CA 95452
(707) 833-6131
www.the-wine-room.com
Multi-winery Tasting, 11-5 Daily

Moshin Vineyards
10295 Westside Road, Healdsburg, CA 95448
(707) 433-5499 or (888) 466-7446
www.moshinvineyards.com
moshin@moshinvineyards.com
Tasting, 11-4:30 Daily
Tours by appointment

Mueller Winery
6301 Starr Road., Windsor, CA 95492
(707) 837-7399
www.muellerwine.com
info@muellerwine.com
Tasting by appointment

Nalle Winery
2383 Dry Creek Road, Healdsburg, CA 95448
(707) 433-1040
www.nallewinery.com
info@nallewinery.com
Tasting, 12-5 Sat, or Sun-Fri by appointment

Papapietro Perry Winery
4791 Dry Creek Road, Healdsburg, CA 95448
(707) 433-0422 or (877) 467-4668
www.papapietro-perry.com
info@papapietro-perry.com
Tasting, 11–4:30 Daily

Peterson Winery
4791 Dry Creek Road Bldg #7, Healdsburg, CA 95448
(707) 431-7568
www.petersonwinery.com
friends@petersonwinery.com
Tours & Tasting by appointment

Petroni Vineyards
990 Cavedale Road, Sonoma, CA 95476
(707) 935-8311 or (888) 290-9390
www.petronivineyards.com
wine@petronivineyards.com
Tasting by appointment, 11-4 Mon-Fri, 10-12 Sat

Pezzi King Vineyards
241 Center Street, Healdsburg, CA 95448
(707) 431-9388 or (800) 411-4758
www.pezziking.com
crowe@pezziking.com
Tasting by appointment

Philip Staley Vineyards & Winery
P.O. Box 1657, Healdsburg, CA 95448
(707) 431-1291
www.staleywines.com

Porter Creek Vineyards
8735 Westside Road, Healdsburg, CA 95448
(707) 433-6321
www.portercreekvineyards.com
info@portercreekvineyards.com
Tasting, 10:30-4:30 Daily

Quivira Vineyards
4900 W. Dry Creek Road, Healdsburg, CA 95448
(707) 431-8333 or (800) 292-8339
www.quivirawine.com
quivira@quivirawine.com
Tasting, 11-5 Daily

Rabbit Ridge Vineyards & Winery
3291 Westside Road, Healdsburg, CA 95448
(707) 431-7128
www.rabbitridgewinery.com
Tasting, 11-5 Daily

Robledo Family Winery
21901 Bonness Road, Sonoma, CA 95476
(707) 939-6903
www.robledofamilywinery.com
Tasting, 10-5 Mon-Sat, 11-4 Sun

Roche Carneros Estate Winery
28700 Arnold Drive, Sonoma, CA 95476
(707) 935-7115 or (800) 825-9475
www.rochewinery.com
info@rochewinery.com
Tasting, 10-5 Daily Winter, 10-6 Daily Summer

J Rochioli Vineyards & Winery
6192 Westside Road, Healdsburg, CA 95448
(707) 433-3205
Tasting, 11-4 Daily

Russian Hill Estate Winery
4525 Slusser Road, Windsor, CA 95492
(707) 575-9428
www.russianhillestate.com
Tasting, 10-4 Thurs-Mon

Sebastiani Vineyards & Winery
389 Fourth Street East, Sonoma, CA 95476
(800) 888-5532 or (707) 933-3230
www.sebastiani.com
info@sebastiani.com
Tasting, 10–5 Daily

Seghesio Family Vineyards
14730 Grove Street, Healdsburg, CA 95448
(707) 433-3579 or (866) 734-4374
www.seghesio.com
Tasting, 10-5 Daily

St. Francis Winery & Vineyards
100 Pythian Road, Santa Rosa, CA 95409
(707) 833-0242 or (800) 543-7713
www.stfranciswinery.com
info@stfranciswinery.com
Tasting, 10-5 Daily; Tours by appointment

Stryker Sonoma Winery & Vineyards
5110 Highway 128, Geyserville, CA 95441
(707) 433-1944 or (800) 433-1944
www.strykersonoma.com
info@strykersonoma.com
Tasting, 10:30-5 Daily

Stuhlmuller Vineyards
4951 West Soda Rock Lane, Healdsburg, CA 95448
(707) 431-7745
www.stuhlmullervineyards.com
info@stuhlmullervineyards.com
Tasting by appointment

Taft Street Winery
2030 Barlow Lane, Sebastopol, CA 95472
(707) 823-2049 or (800) 334-8238
www.taftstreetwinery.com
tastingroom@taftstreetwinery.com
Tasting, 11-4 Mon-Fri, 11-4:30 Sat-Sun

Talty Vineyards & Winery
7127 Dry Creek Road, Healdsburg, CA 95448
(707) 433-8438
www.taltyvineyards.com
mtalty@taltyvineyards.com
Tasting by appointment

Toad Hollow Vineyards
4024 Westside Road, Healdsburg, CA 95448
(707) 431-1441
www.toadhollow.com
info@toadhollow.com
Tasting Room:
409A Healdsburg Avenue, Healdsburg, CA 95448
(707) 431-8667
Tasting, 10:30-5:30 Daily

Wilson Winery
1960 Dry Creek Road, Healdsburg, CA 95448
(707) 433-4355
www.wilsonwinery.com
info@wilsonwinery.com
Tasting, 11-5 Daily

The Wine Room
9575 Sonoma Highway, Kenwood, CA 95452
(707) 833-6131
www.the-wine-room.com
sales@the-wine-room.com
Multi-winery Tasting, 11-5 Daily

Yoakim Bridge Vineyards & Winery
7209 Dry Creek Road, Healdsburg, CA 95448
(707) 433-8511
www.yoakimbridge.com
virginia@yoakimbridge.com
Tasting, 11-4:30 Fri-Sun, or by appointment

Mural inspired by the winery dogs of
Sebastiani Vineyards & Winery

Resident feline at Moshin Vineyards

Max & Sunny shaking off after a swim
Larson Family Winery

Goober saying hello
Benziger Family Winery

"Queen" Rubee
Sebastiani Vineyards & Winery

Sketcher barrel tasting
Chateau Felice

Moose with some of B.R. Cohn's smallest visitors

One of the Watusi cattle at
Gundlach Bundschu

Bodie & Milo dressed for Halloween
A. Rafanelli Winery
photo courtesy of Shelly Rafanelli

Tiny Lily waiting to go outside
Homewood Winery

Amy the resident rooster at
MacMurray Ranch

Muki with winery friend John Scherer
Christopher Creek Winery

Finnegan rules the roost at
Taft Street Winey

Friends and family at Kendall-Jackson

Winery Dogs friend Jennifer Gallegos and our
tiniest helper, Mr. Tea at
Moshin Vineyards

Feline friend at
Johnson's Alexander Valley Wines

Scenic Russian River Valley

Acknowledgments

*Honorary winery dog, Sophie, of Sophie's Cellars
Sonoma Wine and Cheese Market with proprietors David Defries &
John Haggard*

A million thanks to all who have supported our project, from family and old friends to the new faces we've been lucky to meet along the way. Special thanks to David & John for winery suggestions and an endless supply of bread, cheese and words of encouragement, Kyla & John for a lovely stay in Monte Rio, Jenn G. for "working the dogs," Ron for a keen eye, and lastly our families, for their support and critiques throughout the project.